W9-BNS-828

WOMEN *of* COURAGE

INTIMATE STORIES FROM AFGHANISTAN

WOMEN *of* COURAGE
INTIMATE STORIES FROM AFGHANISTAN

KATHERINE KIVIAT + SCOTT HEIDLER

Gibbs Smith, Publisher

TO ENRICH AND INSPIRE HUMANKIND

Salt Lake City | Charleston | Santa Fe | Santa Barbara

This book is for

A young girl named Parwana who embraces all that the future holds
for every woman of Afghanistan, young and old.

Our families and our Afghan "family," the Akbars, who believed in us and this book.
Our circle of friends in Kabul who were always there when we needed them.

🦋

Gibbs Smith, Publisher will donate 5% of net receipts to Mercy Corps' programs in
Afghanistan. For more information on Mercy Corps, please visit www.mercycorps.org

First Edition

11 10 09 08 07   5 4 3 2 1

Text © 2007 Scott Heidler
Photographs © 2007 Katherine Kiviat

All rights reserved. No part of this book may be reproduced by any means whatsoever without
written permission from the publisher, except brief portions quoted for purpose of review.

Published by
Gibbs Smith, Publisher
P.O. Box 667
Layton, Utah 84041

Orders: 1.800.835.4993
www.gibbs-smith.com

Designed by Matthew McNerney / Polemic Design
Printed and bound in China

Library of Congress Cataloging-in-Publication Data
Kiviat, Katherine.
Women of Courage : Intimate Stories from Afghanistan / Katherine Kiviat
and Scott Heidler ; photographs by Katherine Kiviat. — 1st ed.
    p. cm.
  ISBN-13: 978-1-4236-0253-8
  ISBN-10: 1-4236-0253-6
1. Women—Afghanistan—Interviews. 2. Women—Afghanistan—Social conditions.
3. Women—Afghanistan—Pictorial works. I. Heidler, Scott. II. Title.

HQ1735.6.Z75A34 2007
305.48'8915930090511—dc22

2007007939

HARRISON COUNTY
PUBLIC LIBRARY
105 North Capitol Ave.
Corydon, IN 47112
DISCARD

Parwana

CONTENTS

A LONG WAY, BUT THE JOURNEY NOT DONE.

WE all remember those stomach-turning television news images of Afghan women wearing robin's egg blue, all-covering burkas executed in the Kabul stadium—their bodies falling limp and the dust kicking up on the dry field from the exiting bullet. Or we heard the stories of women being beaten on the streets of Afghanistan for infractions that seem frivolous to a Westerner—letting their hair be seen or leaving their family compound without permission.

These images were then countered in late 2001 by those of Afghan women rushing to beauty salons to coif their hair, and little girls wearing crisp new uniforms streaming into classrooms—the first time for most of them going to lessons outside underground, secret schools. All this because of the quick overthrow of the Taliban just months after the terrorist attacks on September 11, 2001.

These are dramatic changes. One day no sunlight and the next what would seem to be free run. What is the situation like for the women of Afghanistan after the world's attention has left? It's a quick turn from public executions to the freedom to learn; is life back to what most in the world would call normal? Who is pushing for continued reform? Who are the women leaders in Afghanistan?

We get the answers to these questions by hearing from the women of Afghanistan. Not from experts, not from journalists, not from humanitarian workers, but from them—the women who are agents of change in their future, in their country.

THE WOMEN OF COURAGE

The lives of Afghan women are changing, but it's not a uniform wave sweeping across the country from the snowcapped Hindu Kush Mountains in the north to the parched Margow Desert in the south. The change is more like a peppering of water springs sprouting from the actions of courageous women across this nation that has seen oppression, death, and destruction for nearly three decades.

Women in urban areas, particularly in the capital Kabul, have many more resources than those in the rural areas. Thus there is a common theme from those seeking a better situation for all Afghan women—the focus needs to be on the rural women for lasting change to truly take hold.

And the change they speak of is not major and progressive like wide acceptance of "love" marriages or women opening businesses. It's baseline change such as educating women—and men—about the rights women now hold in the post-Taliban era. The rights allowing them to leave their family compound to attend school and to shop, and most importantly, to experience a glimmer of independence.

The six years of Taliban rule was not only a black mark for the women of Afghanistan, but for the women of the world. But when the Taliban was overthrown, not all Afghan women ran into the streets ripping their burkas off—and some never will. There are still many cases of abuse, suicide, oppression, attacks on girls' schools, and forced marriage going on even without the oppressive rule of the Taliban. Much work still lies ahead.

That said, Afghan women and girls are seeing a life today they thought impossible during those black days of the Taliban. In the dark corners of a refugee camp near Kabul, in the fields of Bamiyan, and in the dusty offices of Kandahar—the women see a bright future.

They see hope in the positive changes that have taken place, but recognize how fragile those changes are—not that long before the dramatic shift that brought the Taliban to power, women wore miniskirts in Kabul. Afghan women who have been around for thirty years know only too well that as quickly as the situation for women can improve, it can also regress.

With the courage of Afghan heroines from many walks of life—privileged/poor, educated/simple, athletic/disabled, politically connected/rural, self-promoting/motherly—change is taking flight. Hatching from unexpected places, like a butterfly from its cocoon or, in the Dari language, a parwana.

It is here, in the pages of *Women of Courage*, where you will look into the eyes and read the words of some of these heroines. Three have fallen victim since their portraits were taken and their interviews conducted. Victim to the very aspects of life in Afghanistan they were fighting to change.

Shaima Razayee (*page 52*), cohost of *Hop*, an Afghan television music show, was shot dead in her Kabul home in May 2005. She was twenty-four years old. Before she was killed, Shaima believed her life was in danger—receiving death threats for the clothing she wore and how she presented herself on *Hop*. She was fired from the program soon after the conservative Afghan Supreme Court deemed the program "un-Islamic."

Amid rumors of an "honor killing," no one was ever charged in Shiama's death.

Lailama Nabizada (*page 96*), Afghan National Army helicopter pilot, died while giving birth to her first child in July 2006. She was thirty-six years old. After her death, the army now only has one female pilot, her sister Latifa. Maternal mortality is one of the leading causes of death in Afghanistan. According to UNICEF, more than forty percent of deaths among women of childbearing age are caused by preventable complications during pregnancy.

Safia Amma Jan (*page 77, 79*), head of Kandahar Women's Affairs Office, was gunned down by suspected Taliban insurgents as she rode in a cab on her way to work in September 2006. She was sixty-five. Her requests to the provincial government for bodyguards went unanswered. She was killed on the way to her job of forty-four years, fighting the uphill battle for women's rights in a society she loved dearly.

These forty stories from the women of *Women of Courage* are a few of many like them across Afghanistan. It is their brave and selfless actions, and the others out there like them, that will fuel the change for the Afghan woman. Changing the minds of their fellow womankind of the value and power they hold, but also changing the minds of the men of their country to fully open the potential of Afghanistan by allowing all of her people to contribute to her success.

THE BIRTH OF THE BOOK

Prior to hatching the idea for *Women of Courage*, Katherine and I had already been swept off our feet by Afghanistan. She had worked for a nonprofit media organization in Kabul training Afghan women to become photojournalists. I had worked for a humanitarian organization writing articles and taking photos, mostly down in Helmand and Kandahar provinces—then later a freelance journalist traveling all over the country.

We met in New York just a few months before the U.S. invaded Iraq in 2003 and it was because of Afghanistan that we met. A mutual friend introduced us. I had just come back from Afghanistan and Katherine was just on her way. Well, as they say, the rest is history. We have been together ever since, even if not always in the same place.

In March of 2003, I headed to report from Kuwait and Katherine headed to Kabul to teach and to photograph. We spoke frequently—me about running to the basement of the hotel for gas attack sirens, and her about Katyusha rockets falling in the capital. At the end of every conversation, we dreamt about where and when we would meet up. We talked about the fresh food we would eat and how fluffy the pillows would be. When Baghdad fell, that meeting was delayed. I was sent up to Iraq just days after the statue of Saddam Hussein was pulled from its pedestal in the center of the city. I could see the vacant cement platform from my hotel window.

Hearing Katherine tell me how much she had fallen in love with Afghanistan reminded me just how much I missed it. Our meeting with the fluffy pillows and fresh food ended up being in Kabul. I left Baghdad and joined Katherine there …and the food was not fresh nor the pillows fluffy, but it was exactly where we wanted to be.

It was then in the sticky and dusty August of Kabul that the *Women of Courage* idea was born. We thought, how better to help change the situation and perception about Afghan women than to hear stories, from their mouths, of how some women are changing their lives and those around them.

Katherine took a student in her photojournalism class under her wing. Zubaida was special and had a spark that seemed unlikely coming from a slight fifteen-year-old Afghan girl.

It was through her that we met the Akbar family. Zubaida's mother was one of the first subjects (*Azima Nabi, page 50*) of the book and it is her youngest sister Parwana that this book is dedicated to. We felt that she represented the generation of girls who will benefit from the tough and hard-fought changes Afghan women are enduring.

So with Zubaida and her eldest sister Shaharzad on the team, we embarked on the journey to speak with women from across Afghanistan. Our first version of the book was called *Parwana* and published in the two main languages of Afghanistan, Dari and Pashtu, and distributed to all girls' high schools and many women's centers across the country. It has been helping those women and girls out there understand they can do more with their lives—and providing them with examples for inspiration.

Even with all the challenges that lie ahead for Afghanistan, it's not difficult to feel some of the progress. This struck me as Katherine shot photos and I interviewed one of the first two female Afghan Olympians. Yes, because it was mind-blowing that this country was sending two females to represent the country for the very first time, but it was more because of where the photos were shot and the interview conducted. That same stadium. The very same place where women were executed just several years before. ∎

PORTRAITS

16 ·

Overleaf: **Homaira Habib**, Radio Journalist

حميرا حبيب

HOMAIRA HABIB, RADIO JOURNALIST

"I am hopeful that soon there will be a day when men and women in all of Afghanistan, from all walks of life, stand side by side."

What are you teaching in your education radio program? Most of it focuses on how to teach and treat children. We also teach women about their rights, both in Islam and human rights; how they can work outside of the home and problems that they may face.

Do you think this is an important job, educating women about their rights? After so many years of war, many Afghan women do not know about their rights so it is the duty of journalists in Afghanistan to teach the women their rights. This is especially important for us, as we are a radio station for women. We reach half of the women in the city of Herat.

What do you think the future holds for the women of Afghanistan? I am happy with the way the situation is going for women here. I am proud that now just a few years after the Taliban time when women had very few rights, many women are holding high positions in the government, even governor. I am hopeful that soon there will be a day when men and women in all of Afghanistan, from all walks of life, stand side by side.

What do you say to young girls when they tell you that they want to be a journalist like you? I think the most important way to help Afghan women is to educate them and working as a journalist at a women's radio station is the best way to do this. It is also important that these words come from another Afghan woman. This is our responsibility to educate our sisters. We need more women to do this, so whenever any girl asks me about this job I tell them to come and learn, as this is very important work for the future of our country.

What needs to change in the minds of Afghan men so that women in this country can reach their potential? Some Afghan men violate Islamic rules, because they don't know them or they ignore them. Islam gives women rights, but in many places in Afghanistan they don't have those rights. In Islam, women are given the right to go outside and work, to learn and to take part in teaching their children. Some men in Afghanistan don't respect this. If Afghan men learn more about the rights women should have, things will get better.

If you had the choice to leave the country and live an easier life, would you leave Afghanistan? I would not leave. I prefer to stay and work with and for my people. When we lived outside of Afghanistan in the past, I suffered a lot. I would much rather be with my people and working for them.

· 17

HARRISON COUNT
PUBLIC LIBRAR'
105 North Capitoi
Corydon, IN 47112

18 ·

Hanifa Jamizada, Presidential Election Worker

Freeshta Sadat, Abused Wife

حنیفه جامی زاده

HANIFA JAMIZADA, PRESIDENTIAL ELECTION WORKER

"We need to focus on the small changes for women before we take on the challenges the big changes will bring."

20 ·

One of the first tests for women in post-Taliban Afghanistan was the presidential election of 2004. Some women were worried about voting because they were concerned about what people thought. Were you not worried? Worrying is for the women who stay at home and do not go outside; for me that was not a problem. I am educated and I work outside of the home with both men and women, so it's not a problem for me.

What about the rest of your family, including your teenage son; were they worried? No, they had no problems and were very supportive. I was working with the election committee here in Kabul; in the girls' section of a high school that was responsible for distributing the registration cards to the girls.

Did most of the girls at this high school register and vote? Yes, most of the girls did get the registration cards and cast their ballots. I can't say that was the case in all schools, but here it was the case.

There was a woman running for president. She did not win, but if she did what do you think it would have been like—is Afghanistan ready for a woman president? She would not be able to control the government. In Afghanistan the woman is not yet in the role of power, so no one would listen to her. For instance, if I want to change the color of my house I can't do it without the permission of my husband. We need to focus on the small changes for Afghan women before we take on the challenges the big changes will bring.

There still needs to be big changes you say, but is it true that there have been some changes for women since the Taliban were overthrown? The situation now is close to how it was during the time when President Najibullah was ruling the country, but even then the situation was not great for women. And this is just in the major cities. In the villages it is how it has always been; the women are still in the backyard.

If your daughter Helay, who is now thirteen years old, was old enough to vote, would you have encouraged her to vote? I would have told her to vote, because her voice might have an impact on the betterment of the country.

How would you react if Helay had the opportunity to go overseas for study or work? If anyone in my family has the opportunity to leave Afghanistan and live in a developed country, I would tell them to go. But I would make sure that they would never forget their country, their culture, and their religion.

FREESHTA SADAT, ABUSED WIFE

"I hope that men and women will do the same work and get treated as equals and not have any single person rule the life of another."

How do you feel being back home with your mom and dad? It's been two months since I fled my husband and I'm very happy to be back with my family.

Do you not want to be with your husband, or did you simply want to leave his village? I want to be in Kabul with my husband. I don't want to live with my husband's family. It's a very abusive situation.

Why can't this happen? Before he was a Taliban and now he is afraid to live in Kabul.

So you still love your husband and still want to be with him, but you don't want to live with his family? I do still love him, but I want to live with him here in this house with my family in Kabul. I am worried that if a divorce happens then I will lose my daughter. I don't want that to happen at any cost.

Your marriage was forced and now you love your husband, but you don't like this situation, correct? I am forced to be with him now because I am a mother. I will do anything to be with my daughter. I am forced to live this life because I want to be with my daughter.

What do you hope comes out of this *jirga* **(meeting) when the two families meet?** They have accused me of leaving my family and we have accused them of abusing me. We are asking that he moves here to Kabul to live here, and if he does not agree we will get a divorce.

But won't you lose your daughter if you get a divorce? As part of the agreement, my daughter will live with me for three years and then live with his family if I divorce him. If he divorces me, I will get her for six years and have to pay back all the expenses of the wedding.

This is a brave thing for you to do. Most women in your shoes would just stay in their current situation and not do anything. Where have you gotten your bravery? I knew that I had the support of my father and after time I just could not live there anymore, so I just took my daughter and left. I know that this is a bad thing to do in my culture, but I could not take it anymore. I had to leave.

Were you scared when you left? No, I was not afraid. The village I was living in is very remote. I was very lucky and found a car going in the direction of Kabul. I arrived with just my daughter and the clothes on our backs.

What do you hope is different about your daughter's life than that of yours? I want her to live a life very different than mine. I want her to choose whom she marries and I want her to go to school.

If you could change one thing for the women in Afghanistan what would it be? I hope that men and women will do the same work and get treated as equals and not have any single person rule the life of another.

22 ·

Nadera, Bread Maker

نادره

NADERA, BREAD MAKER

"Things are moving forward, but don't leave behind those who still suffer from the past."

What did you do at the bakery? I was part of a work program for women run by Massouda Jalal, the former Minister of Women's Affairs, but then she was working for World Food Program. This was during the Taliban time when women could not work outside of the home.

Where were these bakery shops? They were in another woman's house.

What do you do now for a living? I have gone back to the World Food Program to find a job, but there is nothing for me. I am now trying to get a job.

What kind of work are you looking for now, do you want to go back to being a baker or something different? I would like to work in an office, but I can't read or write so I will have to go back to working in a bakery.

How do you feel about your future, do you think you will learn how to read and write and then get a better job? I can't know before something happens. I hope that I can become literate; I hope that I can get a better job and then a better life, but I don't know if that will happen until it happens.

How do you feel about the future of all Afghan women? Things are getting better, girls are going to school and that will help them have a better future. And having educated women can only help all of Afghanistan in the future.

Let's look at your current situation; if you were not prevented from going to school during the Taliban time, you could have an office job right now. Do you encourage other girls to go to school, now that they can? It is very important that all young girls go to school. Because I did not go to school, I don't have a good job. I tell them this and encourage them to go to school. I tell them to look at me, I will never get any other work than in a bakery so they should go to school and learn as much as they can. This will help them have a better future.

Now that there is a new path for Afghan women, what needs to change right now, what is most important? I think that the government should do something for the women who are illiterate. Make programs like factory work or something like this, so those who can't read or write can feed their family. Things are moving forward, but don't leave behind those who still suffer from the past.

"For the first time in a long time all the people of Afghanistan have their eyes open, they know what needs to be done for a good future."

— Jamila Mujahid, TV Journalist

Jamila Mujahid, TV Journalist

Shaima Rahmany, Filmmaker

JAMILA MUJAHID, TV JOURNALIST

"For the first time in a long time all the people of Afghanistan have their eyes open, they know what needs to be done for a good future."

How long have you been a journalist? It has been twenty-four years that I have been working at Afghan Radio and Television. I started working on the children's program and have been with them ever since.

Were you still working during the Taliban time? During the Taliban time, I did not leave Kabul. I stayed in my home and suffered in many ways. I was the first woman journalist to announce the fall of the Taliban and for this I have won a journalistic award.

Where were you when you reported the fall of the Taliban? Right here where I have always worked, Afghan Radio and Television. Because I was in such a rush to get here and report, I did the broadcast with my slippers on my feet and had to wear a burka to get to the studio. One week after this broadcast, we restarted the news operation.

How long had it been since you did your last broadcast before this historic reporting? There was a very bad situation here in Kabul for ten years before, so this was the first broadcast I had done in over a decade.

This historic broadcast must have been amazing for you for two reasons—one, because you were not allowed to do your job during the rule of the Taliban and two, because this was a very big moment for your country. How did that make you feel? It was always my dream to give the announcement of freedom to the people of Afghanistan. I now thank God that I can see these days of freedom for my fellow country people.

A TV journalist is a difficult job for a woman in any country. To what can you credit your success in Afghanistan—probably the most difficult place for a woman to have your job? I had always had the interest and drive to do this. My family and husband were always by my side supporting me in this career.

Your dedication is something to admire. What advice do you give Afghan women who want to be like you, maybe not the exact profession, but women who want to pursue their dreams? Every time I am with Afghan women I encourage them to get an education and go to school and, most importantly, understand their rights as an Afghan woman. Also, that they need to support and promote freedom and liberty.

How do you see the future for women in Afghanistan? I am hopeful for two reasons. For the first time in a long time all the people of Afghanistan have their eyes open, they know what needs to be done for a good future. We have all experienced war and we know what we have to do to prevent more war. And the second reason is that now the world—after a very long time—is paying attention to us, to my country Afghanistan.

شیما رحمانی

SHAIMA RAHMANY, FILMMAKER

"Men and women need to talk to each other more. If there is respect between the two, then there will not be a problem."

Many Afghan people think that making films is not an honorable profession for a woman. Why do you do it? It is difficult. I had problems with my family when I told them what I wanted to do. But it is what I really want to do, so I do it.

What did your family say? My mother and father were fine with it; it was my uncles and aunts who did not want me to do this. They have stopped coming to see my family. They have broken communication off with my immediate family.

How does this make you feel? I don't care because I like my job. I have to think of what I want to do. I have to live my life and I can't allow other people to control my life. I respect my relatives and I listen to what they say, but if they are trying to stop me from improving myself I will do it anyway.

Are you married? No, and I will only get married if I find a man who will accept me and what I do for a living. If not, I will not get married. It is difficult because sometimes a man will agree to a woman who is working in film but his family will not. This is a new situation in Herat, so it is difficult for them to accept this.

What do you tell young girls who tell you that this is what they want to do for a living? It is difficult to make films now, but Afghanistan will change. I tell them that they should start to do this now as I think it will become more socially accepted for women to act in and produce films. If they get the experience now, they will be much more successful when the people of Afghanistan realize the importance of film.

What is the single thing that needs to change right now? I want more freedom for women. It does not really matter what they wear, but what is important is the freedom to work and to do what they want. Their families should learn to trust them more. If they are working, they are doing good things for themselves as well as for their family.

What needs to change with Afghan men so women can reach their potential? The men need to know the rights of women and how to treat their wives with respect. The same goes for women; they should know their husband and what he wants and respect his wishes. Men and women need to talk to each other more. If there is respect between the two, then there will not be a problem.

34 ·

شگوفه سحر

SHAGOOFA SAHAR, HOST OF *GOOD MORNING AFGHANISTAN* RADIO SHOW

"I think that my work is an encouragement for Afghan children that they can do many things with their lives."

Three years ago, you would never have been able to do this kind of work. How do you feel about what you do now? I am very happy to be able to do this kind of work and I think that it is an encouragement for children in Afghanistan that they can do many things with their lives.

You are doing something that very few twelve-year-old girls would be doing. What do you tell the girls who ask how they can do this work? I tell them that they should always be learning, and being on radio I am always learning. This is the key to a better life, education.

Was your family supportive of you taking this job? My parents were very happy and encouraged me to take this radio job. They saw it as a way to improve myself and help the children of Afghanistan and my society.

You have interviewed President Hamid Karzai. How did that feel sitting across from him and interviewing him? I was delighted that I had this opportunity to talk with him. I never dreamt that a president would take the time to speak with the children of his country and talk about the problems that they are facing.

What did you talk about? We talked about the needs of the children and that it is very important to study, but also about the need for children to be children, to have fun and be entertained.

Do you see yourself as an advocate for the rights of Afghan children? I see this as my job. The children of Afghanistan will make the future of this country, so it is very important to me that I work for their well-being and their rights.

How do you see the future for Afghan girls? If we get help from outside countries and our leaders work very hard for the country, and for nothing else but to make Afghanistan better, I think there will be many positive changes here.

What else do you do, outside of your job, to help the Afghan children? At school, I encourage my fellow students to continue with their studies, and to listen to training programs on the radio and to focus on their future.

What do you see for yourself in the future? I would like to be president and serve the Afghan people the best way that I can.

If you could sit across the table from a twelve-year-old girl living in the West, what would you say to her? I would say to her that even though your country is very developed and you have many facilities it's good to focus on education. This is the most important thing for children who live anywhere in the world.

جنرال خاتول محمد زی

GENERAL KHATOOL MUHAMMAD ZAI, AFGHAN ARMY PARATROOPER

"Women are playing a role in helping Afghanistan, with or without the burka on."

How long were you a paratrooper? Twenty years.

Why did you decide to join the military, was it just to jump out of planes? I'm an athletic woman and I was drawn to a career that used physical activity and I have always been interested in airplanes and skydiving.

What happened during the Taliban time? Were you able to still be in the military and be a paratrooper? When the Taliban took control no women could even go outside, really. I acted like all of the other women and stayed inside, sewing at home. I did not forget about my job; I drew things about my job.

When was the last time you jumped? The last time I jumped was Mujaheddin Freedom Day. There are three major Afghan holiday celebrations—Afghan Freedom Day, New Year's Day, and Mujaheddin Freedom Day. Now that the Taliban is gone, we have a military display for these holidays.

What do you tell the young Afghan women who approach you and say they want to be like you? I tell them to do everything on their own and be honest when they deal with all people. They should not stray from their aim and should not do anything that might compromise that goal. They need to do everything on their own if they want to have a high position like president. But most importantly, they should just be honest.

Do you want to run for president, make it President Khatool instead of General Khatool? If it's God's will I will become president, but there are many qualified people out there who can do a good job now. I think it is important for me to keep my current job and do well at what I am doing now. If people want me to run I will run, but not now. If God wills it.

What do you see as the future for the women of Afghanistan? Women are making breakthroughs, but isn't there a great deal that still needs to be done? If Afghan women have good jobs with good pay it will bring women back to Afghanistan who have left, bringing a much stronger voice for the Afghan woman. In the world right now there is a golden opportunity for some women, but Afghan women have a diamond opportunity. If they use this opportunity, they can do anything.

Even now some parts of the Afghan community are not open to the evolving role and position of women, do you see that changing anytime soon? For example, some families are still forcing women to wear burkas...will that change anytime soon? Improving the economic situation here can help the women who have to provide for their family on their own. Some of the women wear burkas because they are so poor that they are embarrassed of their clothes and cover them up with a burka. If the economy improves, they can buy clothes that they are proud of and not wear burkas. But the main point is that women are playing a role in helping Afghanistan, with or without the burka on. Security is also very important to them. For the burka, it is important to do what their culture says, or the culture they believe in. Every culture in the world does different things. I can't tell them that they should wear burkas or that they should not. What I can say is that Afghan women should be working.

Kabul Police Academy shooting practice for female officers at a shooting range outside Kabul, Afghanistan.

Fariba Razayee, Afghan Judo Olympian

Naheed Mirza, Police Academy Graduate

فریبا رضایی

"Even though I did not win at the Olympics, I achieved something by teaching women in Afghanistan about what they can do."

42 ·

Representing Afghanistan in the Athens Olympics is a very big accomplishment for you. How did it make you feel? Going to Greece taught me a great deal about competing. All of us who went to the Olympics from Afghanistan tried our very best so that more athletes from our country can go to future games.

You were one of the first two women to represent your country. How did that make you feel? I was proud to represent my country. It was important to show the world that Afghan women can be athletes, and also to show the people in my country that Afghan women can compete with other countries of the world.

What example are you setting for Afghan women? I showed them that they can do many things and break out of the thinking that they only have few rights. They can do anything they want to and they can be athletes not only in Afghanistan, but share the athletic field with women from around the world.

Just going to the Olympics made you a winner, but how did you feel when you lost your competition? When I lost at the Olympics, I was crying and very sad. Just twenty minutes after my competition, my father called me. I was crying, but he told me not to cry or be sad. He said that this was like the first step on the moon and said, "You are my champion."

What kind of difficulties have you come across being a female athlete? There have been very difficult times for me and for my family. For instance, when I was leaving for training before the Olympics my mother's friends were asking her how she could let me go. When I came back, so many things had changed. Those women met me with flowers and gifts and told me how proud they were.

How does it make you feel that you have changed people's minds? It was even surprising to me when I came back. Like these women, to see how they changed their minds and now they even want to let their own daughters go into sports.

What do you think the future holds for the women of Afghanistan? It depends on the women of Afghanistan. They are the only ones who can stand on their own feet and decide what kind of future they want. They are the ones who need to decide their future.

So many women in Afghanistan have never had the opportunity to think for themselves. What kind of encouragement do they need to start exercising their freedom? The most important inspiration for Afghan women is to look at women in other countries, as well as the women in our country, who have done great things. Then they can look at these women and think, "I'm a human, I'm a woman, I have all the rights and I should use them."

ناهید میرزا

NAHEED MIRZA, POLICE ACADEMY GRADUATE

"I will encourage women to follow their hearts and do what they want to do and what makes them happy."

What made you decide to come to the police academy? People who were recruiting for the police academy came to my school. I was very interested after hearing their presentation and I signed up.

Have you faced any resistance or bad reactions from people outside of your family? Some of my female teachers at my school said to me that this was not a good idea.

Why did they say it was not a good idea for you to join the police force? They said to me that Afghanistan is not ready for policewomen, but my family told me not to listen to them. My mother was particularly supportive of my going to the academy.

How did you find the courage to come here? When the women who had already graduated from the police academy came to my school, I really liked how they spoke about their training and how the training came through in the way they carried themselves.

Do you hope you can do the same for other women, set an example and encourage them to go to the academy or do something they never thought they could do? I encourage any woman who asks me about what I'm doing to follow their heart and do what they want to do and what makes them happy.

How does it make you feel when women become interested in what you do? It makes me feel great. More women need to know that this is a good job.

What did it feel like the first time you shot a gun? I was afraid before I shot, but after the first shot I was much more comfortable.

How did you do in shooting the target? Of all the girls, I had the best average.

How did that make you feel? I could not believe that I got the best. I was very surprised.

When the girls in your class were shooting the targets, the boys were laughing. How did that make you feel? Most of the boys—even before shooting practice—were telling us that girls should not be at the police academy, so that's why they were laughing. But once they saw that we could shoot, they stopped laughing right away. After all the shooting was done and we were awarded our positions, the boys came over and congratulated us.

How do you feel about the future for the women of Afghanistan? We can't say what will happen for certain, but I can say that everyone in my country wants a better future.

What do you want to do in the future? I want to be one of the female teachers at the academy.

What happens when you get married? I won't marry a man who won't let me keep my job with the police.

Massouda Jalal, Former Minister of Women's Affairs, Presidential Candidate

Shaharzad Akbar, Kabul University Student

48 ·

Azima Nabi, Teacher and Mother of Six

عظیمه نبی

AZIMA NABI, TEACHER AND MOTHER OF SIX

"Now, all women must make the effort to learn."

How has the situation for Afghan women changed in the last few years? I am very happy that women now have the opportunity to work, go to school, and in a sense have respectable lives, but I hope that all women make the effort to learn. This is the most important freedom for women since the fall of the Taliban. Now, all women must make the effort to learn.

How are you encouraging your daughters to capitalize on the changes for women living in Afghanistan? I only went to school until sixth grade and then stopped because of the fighting during the Soviet occupation. I did not have a mother as she died when I was very small.

My father wanted me to become a doctor, but the school was burned to the ground because of the fighting. So I studied at home and then took an exam. Now the government is making me go to college if I want to continue teaching. I do not want this to be what happens to my daughters. This is why it is important for them to go to school now, before they are married and have a family.

Since it has been so long since women were able to teach, are you facing problems? Many of the women teachers have children and if their children are sick or are young, there is no childcare to help them out. So if they have to stay at home with their children, they cannot teach. And many of the women teachers are leading their families because their husbands have been killed in wars. It's very difficult as the salaries are so low, they can't properly feed their families off just their salaries.

Do you encourage your students, like your daughters, that their future outlook is much different than before? I encourage them very much. I tell them that they will have much more control of their future if they work very hard. I encourage them to continue their studies. It's difficult for some of the older girls because they are discouraged studying with the younger girls. I tell them that they need to continue, because this is their time. This is the time to make the changes in their life that they could not make in the past. I help the older ones make up the grades that they missed during the Taliban time and get to the grades where they should be quicker—making them feel better and more confident.

How do you feel about the future of the women living in Afghanistan? I think the future for women in Kabul is bright, but there are things that need to be done to help them. There should be more basic literacy classes for older women who have to work at home. Some women were never able to learn and some still cannot even leave their homes.

Shaima Razayee, Host, *Hop* Music TV Program

52 .

شیما رضایی

**"I think that there is a bright future for Afghan women
if they find the courage to do new things."**

What kind of reaction do you get from your family about your job? All of them have been very supportive, especially my mother and father.

You are helping to change the role of Afghan women, as your job has really never been realized for a woman. What reaction do you get? At first I had a little bit of trouble because of the way I acted on my program. I laughed and made jokes. I am very happy that I am touching the young people of Afghanistan and am honored when they tell me how much they like the show.

When they tell you that they like you and your program, what do you say to them? I encourage both boys and girls; in fact I have introduced three other music TV hosts to this station, Tolo TV.

What do you think needs to change for women in Afghanistan? I think that more women need to start working. Look at me. I'm a young Afghan woman and I'm working. Others need to ignore the bad things that people say and start working.

The way things are going now, how do you feel about the future for Afghan women? I think that there is a bright future for Afghan women if they find the courage to do new things. They will improve themselves and the situation for all Afghan women if they are courageous and carve new paths.

You and your sister, the judo Olympian Fariba, have set amazing examples for all Afghan women. Is there competition between the two of you? Not really. We are leading very different lives and encourage each other.

It is unique that two very strong-willed and successful girls come from one family. Where did you get the encouragement to pursue this life, this career? Our parents helped us pursue our dreams. They are very supportive and encourage us to go after our dreams and focus on doing what we want to. My one brother was not happy about what I was doing, but my parents told him to let me be my own person and let me go after my dreams. Now he is okay with what I do and he even watches my program.

What's next for you now? I want to continue with this job and become the best at it as I can. After that I want to study more and go to law school. After that I want to get into politics.

Which politicians do you look up to the most? Hamid Karzai, Massouda Jalal, and Suhila Siddiq.

Will you run for office or will you work for a ministry? It's my wish to study hard and then become a minister or maybe even become president.

Miriam Farooq, Language Teacher/Former Underground Teacher

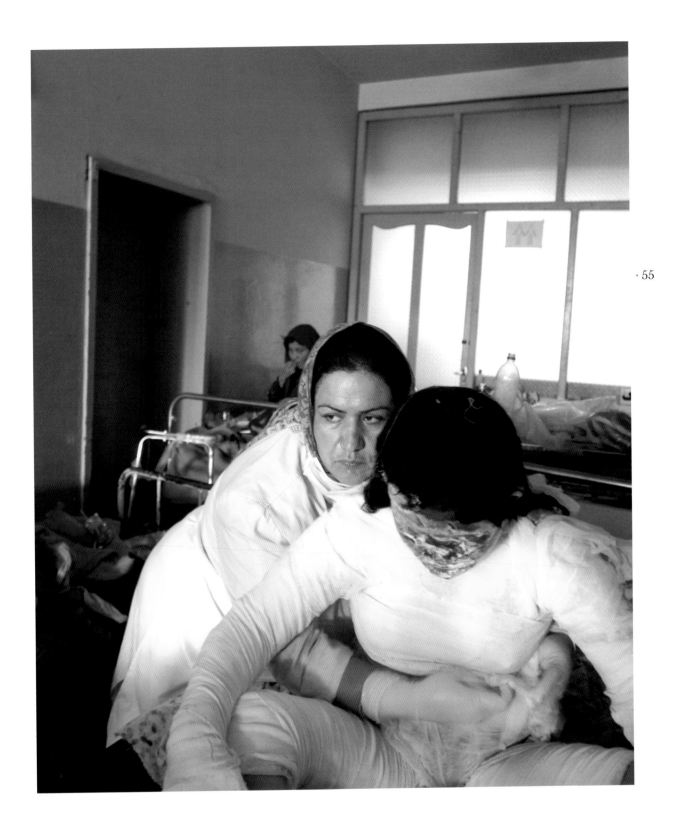

Shaima Aminy, Burn Unit Nurse at Herat Hospital

MIRIAM FAROOQ, LANGUAGE TEACHER/
FORMER UNDERGROUND TEACHER

**"The way the situation needs to change for the women
of Afghanistan is slow and calculated."**

What is the most important aspect of your teachings? I teach girls who are too old to attend school now, but they still want to learn.

So they are girls who missed out on education because they were forbidden to learn during the Taliban time? Yes. They are over the age to go to school, but want to make up for the education they missed. They lost out because the Taliban was ruling the country. I am trying to help them get back on track. Of all of my students, they are the ones working the hardest. They have been denied the right to an education and now they are taking matters into their own hands and learning. I am very proud to be helping each one of them become an active person in the future.

What did you do during the Taliban time? I held secret classes to teach girls. While they were ruling, I wanted to do everything I could to help the girls in my community learn. We did not know what the future held. I thought it was important to prepare as best we could.

Outside of your traditional lessons, what do you teach the girls? I make sure they understand their new rights as women. Many of them were too young during the Taliban to realize that things have now changed.

What is the most important thing you teach them about their rights? That they have the right to better themselves through education. This is something that I, and many other women like me, fought for during the Taliban time. The key for them to progress and have a bright future is to learn.

How do you see your role changing in the future? My job will always be teaching women and girls. This is the primary and necessary step for the women of this country to better themselves. If they are not educated, they will not know their rights. They have to learn to think for themselves and also know how it is for women in other countries.

You have a young daughter, what do you think Afghanistan will be like when she grows up? I want her to start school as early as possible—studying all the way to becoming a doctor. I still have to wear a burka now and then. I want her to never have to wear a burka.

Even though things are changing, not everyone wants the situation for Afghan women to get better. Have you ever faced problems at your school? We had a situation where the students voted that they did not want to wear burkas. This was great to hear as a teacher—they thought about the decision in a democratic way and wanted to move forward, but we had to tell them not to do it. If word got out that all the students stopped wearing burkas because of this vote at school, many parents would stop allowing their daughters to come to classes. The way the situation needs to change for the women of Afghanistan is slow and calculated. There will be problems if things go too fast.

شيما امينى

SHAIMA AMINY, BURN UNIT NURSE AT HERAT HOSPITAL

"We used to have only a few beds, but now we have a whole section of the hospital."

What do you think the future holds for the women of Afghanistan? I have a good feeling about the future. Things are going well and they continue to improve. Over the last three years the situation has become better and Afghanistan is becoming more developed.

With this progress, what is the one thing that still needs to change for women? There is one problem that is still here. Women in educated families are allowed to develop, but women in illiterate families are still struggling.

What can change this, how can illiterate women learn their rights? The leaders of each village need to be told that the women have the right to learn, the right to work outside of the home. This should be done by mullahs because they hold the authority to change the way things are done in the villages. If the people hear this coming from the mullahs, it will happen.

Were more or less women burning themselves during the Taliban? We are seeing many more cases of this now.

Why do you think this is, the situation is better for women in Afghanistan now, but they are still hurting themselves? There are many reasons. Some do this because their husbands have other wives. There are young women who are being forced into marriages with men they don't know. Some are jealous that another girl in her family has married a rich man and she has married a poor man. There are even cases where mothers-in-law make their son's wives burn themselves.

Were there not more reasons for women to hurt themselves during the Taliban time? I'm not sure why more do it now, but there are many more doing it. During the Taliban time, one hundred women would do this per year and now it's five hundred each year. We used to have only a few beds, but now we have a whole section of the hospital. We have to turn women away sometimes because we have no more room.

Why has there been such an increase? Before women did not know their rights. Now they do and they act on the frustration of their lives. Most of them come from uneducated families and when they see educated families allowing their women freedom that the uneducated women don't have, they hurt themselves. During the Taliban all women had no freedom, now only the educated women do.

Do many husbands come to visit the women who burn themselves? The only reason the husbands come here is out of fear. They are afraid that if they do not come and their wife dies, that her family will try to put them in jail or ask for blood money. This is the only reason that they come.

What would you say to a woman who is going to burn herself? Usually a woman has more patience than a man. In their life, they normally will suffer more. My advice to women who are thinking of burning themselves is to wait and think about what will happen if they do this . . . what will happen to their family. They should use their patience and think about what they are going to do. They should know that there is another way. All people have problems, they can figure out another way.

Zahra Mohammadi, Divorcée

زهرا محمدی

ZAHRA MOHAMMADI, DIVORCÉE

"Men's behavior toward women needs to change."

What happened with your marriage? My husband and I had problems from the beginning; he did not like my family. He also ordered me to do many things. One day he asked me to collect dung from our neighbors to burn during the winter. I came from a city, so this was unacceptable to me. We fought after this, after I refused to get the dung. He then told me that it would be better if I killed myself, to burn myself to death.

How did he react when you actually lit yourself on fire? He just looked at me. And when I ran outside screaming, he did nothing but drink tea.

How did your husband treat you before this? He was beating me and used bad words all of the time.

How did your mother react when she saw you after you burned yourself? She did not know what I did when I first saw her. My husband's family made me swear to God not to say anything about what happened.

Was this a forced marriage? It was arranged by my parents. I did not say anything about the marriage at first as we got along fine.

Did he make false promises about the kind of man he was? Yes, the first few days he was pretending to be a good man, but after that I could see the real man that he was.

What would you tell other women who are thinking of burning themselves like you did? I would tell them not to do it. No matter how bad their situation is, it will not be the same as the suffering that I have gone through after burning myself. I am suffering more from burning myself then being married to an abusive husband. And my suffering will last for a long time. It takes a very long time to heal from this. I would tell them to talk to their family and to get help from the government before they do something like this.

If you could talk to a woman right before she was going to burn herself, what would you say? Don't do it. It's not the answer to her problems.

What would you tell all the husbands out there whose wives are thinking of burning themselves? It is their responsibility to treat their wives with respect and not to make their lives so bad that they want to hurt themselves.

What do you think the future holds for the women of Afghanistan? It will be better. It won't get worse than it is now.

There is much progress in Afghanistan. What needs to change right now? The most important things are freedom and independence. Women want to be treated well by their husbands and all men around them. Men's behavior toward women needs to change.

When I was in prison, they burned me with cigarettes, they shocked me with electricity, but nothing will stop me from doing what I am doing.

— Suraya Parlika, Executive Director,
All Afghan Women's Union

ثریا پرلیکا

"When I was in prison, they burned me with cigarettes, they shocked me with electricity, but nothing will stop me from doing what I am doing."

What does your union do? The union started in 1992 when the Mujaheddin entered Kabul. At first it was a secret union as the security was not good for women to go outside and study or go to work. So this union helped Afghan women with courses in basic education, English, and computers. First it was just in Kabul and then in all areas of Afghanistan and then even Pakistan.

What happened during the Taliban time? It continued strongly during the Taliban to help educate women, but to also continue to build a union for women.

What needs to change to get the basics of life back for women? There are lots of women who are begging in the streets, lots of women are living in tents and lots of women have lost their parents, their husbands; they are begging because they don't have anything to eat. I think that more working opportunities need to open up for these women. This helps women in two ways; first, economic independence will stop them from begging, and then it will lead to women living a more independent life.

Your work is risky and it is dangerous to speak the way you do. What inspired you to do it? When I was studying in school I was fortunate to come from a family that had a little bit of money and I would see women and children who had to beg for their food and beg to live. I kept asking why, why, why and what was needed to end this suffering. From these experiences I wanted to focus my life on preventing it.

What kept you working even after someone tried to kill you? I am committed and this was not the first risk I have taken; I am not giving up. I am committed to fighting for the equal rights of the women of Afghanistan. These things won't stop me. When I was in prison, they burned me with cigarettes, they shocked me with electricity, but nothing will stop me from doing what I am doing.

What about your family, what do they think about what you are doing? Are they just as committed? Of course parents worry about their children, and my brother was worrying about me as well. But even in their worry, they never told me to stop what I was doing.

I'm sure many young Afghan women look up to you and to what you have dedicated your life to. What do you tell them when they ask what they can do? Many women talk to me—university students, housewives, many women. The first thing I do is ask them if they know about their rights. And then I encourage them to fight for a government that is not ruled by the gun or by money and I encourage them to work for this so everyone can live safely.

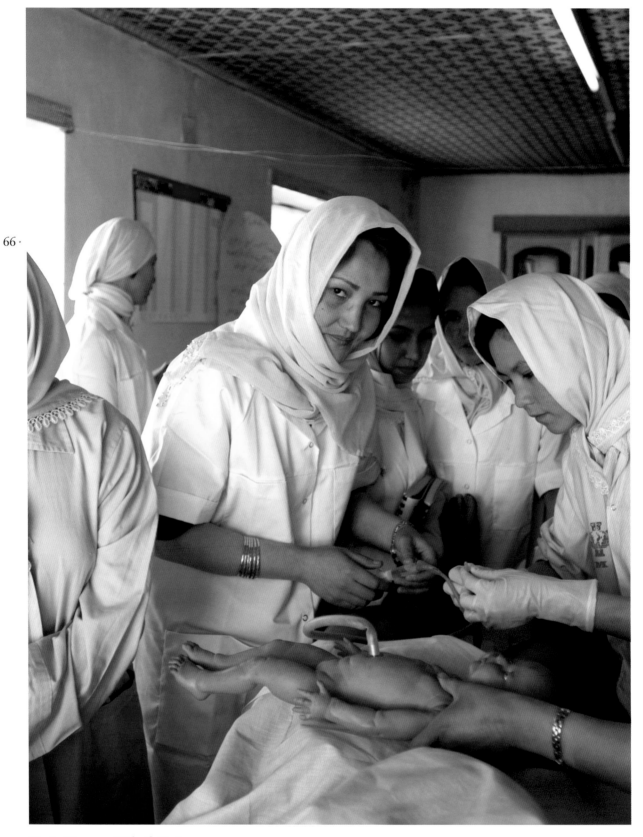

Huria Hessary, Midwife Trainer

Marzia Tamaski, Supermarket Saleswoman

Shazia Saba, Office Manager, Bamiyan DDR (Disarmament, Demobilization and Reintegration)

74 ·

Abeershah, Fortune-Teller

Safia Amma Jan, Head of Women's Affairs Office in Kandahar

عبير شاه

ABEERSHAH, FORTUNE-TELLER

"All of the Afghan women are my sisters, all of the children of Afghanistan are my children."

You have been living here in the rural area of Jawjan for forty-five years, what is your job? I tell the future for girls and boys and open the luck for the people I meet with. My husband died when I was thirty, and I had to take care of my family. That is why I started doing this work, telling people their future.

Are you the only person making money for your family? Yes, I'm the only one who is working. Two of my sons are married but don't have work.

Tell me more about your job. When I was a child I was not well, so my parents went to fortune-tellers to help cure me. I always kept a prayer written on a cloth in my hand at all times, but after the birth of my first son I lost it. When he grew up he died in an airplane accident.

Before that son died, he took me to an important fortune-teller and the man gave me all of his powers. Mostly men taught me how to tell the future and how to help change the luck for girls who want to get married and how to help when people are lost. This is what I do now for people. I help when people need their luck to change.

What do you predict for the future of all women in Afghanistan? Things will get better for Afghan women. The world is developing; Afghanistan is developing. Women are working, they are going to school, but the situation will only continue to get better if our leaders stay on the right path. If they are good the future will be good.

If you had the power to change one thing for the women of your country right now, what would it be? All of the Afghan women are my sisters, all of the children of Afghanistan are my children. I pray for all of them to develop and improve their lives. Freedom is the main thing that needs to change for Afghan women. Some women are starting to travel to other provinces, but many are still forced to stay at home. This is what needs to change now, freedom. Women also need to have more opportunities for jobs. All people, men and women, who are healthy should be working.

During the Taliban, rule if they found out what you were doing they would have killed you; why did you still do it? Because I was hungry, I had to do this. I needed to find money for my family. I also worked in people's houses and cleaned. I worked wherever I could find it.

What needs to change in the way men act toward women? Right now all of my daughters go to school. Their brothers and other male relatives do not prevent them from going to learn. This is good and is the most important change.

صفیه عمه جان

SAFIA AMMA JAN, HEAD OF WOMEN'S AFFAIRS OFFICE IN KANDAHAR

"The people of this community depend on me, so I will never leave. That is why they call me Amma; I am their aunt."

Kandahar is a very conservative area especially when it comes to women's issues. What is the biggest challenge your office here faces? The biggest challenge for us is when women come to us to help improve their life and their family by getting a job. I am so proud that they come to this decision and to us for help, but I am heartbroken when we have nothing for them. When there are no jobs to help them I feel like I have failed.

When there are no jobs available what are you able to do for them? What are some of your successes in this difficult area? Our professional training programs—we have classes that teach women many different trades, like how to work with flowers. We are teaching them things to better their lives, new skills they did not think of before. I feel that this is a success for us because they are learning, but there is something bigger here. These programs are getting the women to come out of their houses. They see hope when they get out of their house. They see that there are many things that they can do and that other women are doing them too.

What is one thing that needs to change for all women of Afghanistan? For the first time in twenty-five years the women of Afghanistan are seeing light again—twenty-five years of war and twenty-five years of staying inside. Now women can come outside and start living their lives again. The most important thing for the women of my country is jobs. The freedoms are slowly expanding, but if they don't have a way to feed their family—what good is that freedom? They all need to find jobs.

How do men need to change to make it better for the women of Afghanistan? They need to become aware of the rights women now have in Afghanistan. Things are changing and the responsibility is on the men to know what has changed—to make it better for their family, but also to make it better for our country. They need to take on the responsibility of this.

How do the men in your life react to your position with the Ministry of Women's affairs? I have been working for the women of my country and for the people of my country for forty-four years. My father gave me the permission when I was a young girl and now my husband allows me to do this. It is who I am. I have been doing this kind of work for so long, the men in my life see it as part of who I am.

If you had a chance to live an easier life outside of Afghanistan, would you go? I stayed here, in my country, during years of war, why would I go now? I love Afghanistan and want to be here to help it become a better place for everyone. I'll stay to make sure that happens. The people of this community depend on me, so I will never leave. That is why they call me Amma; I am their aunt. I am the aunt of Kandahar.

Are you going to retire? I have tried to leave the position, but the position will not let me go. There is too much to do, and I cannot sit back and do nothing.

Mahjan, Housewife

ماه جان

MAHJAN, HOUSEWIFE

"Afghanistan is getting better day by day and I want my children to be prepared for the future when things become even better."

Your daughter Bobani is blind and that must make it very difficult for her. What does she want to do in the future? I make every sacrifice so that she can do anything she wants. She's blind, but she can still do many things. I work very hard at getting her an education and teaching her to stand on her own two feet. I don't want her to have to rely on anyone else.

Does your daughter have more opportunities now than in the past? Once the Taliban left Kabul I focused on educating and preparing my children for the future; making sure that they could have jobs in the future, becoming more independent. Afghanistan is getting better day by day and I want my children to be prepared for the future when things become even better. I don't allow my children to do any work at the house. If they are home, I tell them to study or to read. Now is the time for them to get a better life, so they need to work hard.

Your daughter has a challenging life being blind, but with the way things are changing for women in Afghanistan do you think she will have more opportunities than when you were her age? Yes, the main difference is education. There is such a focus on all children going to school. This is going to be the difference between when I was a child and now for my children. None of our children will have jobs when they are in school. Their job is to learn.

Is your husband supportive of sending all of your children to school? He is very interested that all of our children go to school. He and I agree that this is the key for a better future for them. We think that a person without an education is like a blind person. I am learning at the same time with my children. I was unable to read before, but now I study with my children and I can read now.

You are fortunate that your husband is supportive of educating your entire family. What do you tell women whose husbands don't feel this way and don't allow their daughters to go to school? I tell them that it is our responsibility as parents to make sure that our children live better lives than we did. I even convinced one of my relatives to send her daughter to school. A person who cannot read and write is like a blind person. My blind daughter is even better off than an illiterate person because she can read and write in her own way with braille.

How do you feel about the future for Afghan women? If the peace stays, it will get better day by day. The situation is improving, but it all depends on the peace.

"If you are living your life for just you — you are not living."

— Pashtoon Shahna, Girls' High School Principal

Pashtoon Shahna, Girls' High School Principal

Fatema Kamazemyan, Head of Women's Affairs Office in Bamiyan

PASHTOON SHAHNA, GIRLS' HIGH SCHOOL PRINCIPAL

"If you are living your life for just you—you are not living."

88 ·

What paved the way for the current change the women of Afghanistan are experiencing? I think the first step toward a better future for the women of this country was when the new constitution was approved. Part of that constitution was dedicated to making a brighter future for us.

You are working firsthand with the future women leaders of this country. How have things changed for them here at this school over the last few years? The women of this area are very strong. Even during the time of the Taliban we still ran our schools. We did not care what they thought and we knew that it was very important for our future that we continue educating our girls.

What is the most important thing you can do to change the lives of the girls at this school? The first thing I need to do is make sure all of my teachers have the best and most up-to-date education. If the teachers are not performing to the best of their ability, the students will not learn. And for the women in the community, I go to their houses and help them gain their independence by telling them of their rights.

What is the most important thing for the girls in your school to learn? English. It is now the international language and, for a long time to come, Afghanistan will have people coming here from outside. It is important for our children to be able to communicate with them. Also, you need to know English to use computers in the best possible way.

What needs to change for women right now? Women need to become more involved in our government and run for more offices. If we want to keep the progress we have made for women in this country, and want more progress to come, we need people in the government pushing for it. I plan on running someday myself.

How do men need to change? Women cannot expect men to make changes for them. Women have to go out and change things on their own. We need to fight for our rights. It would be better if men tried to learn a little about what the women are going through in Afghanistan so they could better understand the changes we are asking for.

What do you say to young girls who tell you they want to do what you do? I have always tried to encourage the girls who are my students, but also all the young teachers at this school. Education is an ongoing process—it should never end, as their thirst to learn more should never be quenched. I tell them that the future of our country is up to them. My generation had very difficult times so now it is up to them, the younger generation, to make a good future for Afghanistan.

I also tell them that they should not live their lives just for themselves. Live it for many people, their family and their country; because if you are living your life for just you—you are not living.

فاطمه کاظمیان

FATEMA KAMAZEMYAN, HEAD OF WOMEN'S
AFFAIRS OFFICE IN BAMIYAN

"I will stay here and work for the women of my country as long as I am able to do so."

How do you feel the situation for the women of Bamiyan differs from that of women in other parts of Afghanistan? The social situation for women in Bamiyan is better than any other place in Afghanistan. The greatest number of women registered to vote here during the presidential election. The men and women in Bamiyan are ready for change more than any other province in Afghanistan.

What do you feel the future holds for all the women of Afghanistan? Afghan women have a very bright future; we have both the support of the people of our country and the support of the world. It is also part of our constitution that women have rights. Many countries from around the world are helping the women of Afghanistan and if the women realize that they have so much support, they will go very far.

What needs to be done to change this social structure of men? We need to give more opportunities for women in high positions. When men see that women can perform well in high positions and have power, they will shift their ideas about women. For example, Bamiyan now has a female governor. This will show the men here that women can work and can hold high positions.

What advice do you give young girls who tell you they want to be like you and work for the Ministry of Women's Affairs? I encourage them and tell them that they should find their place within our society and work as hard as they can. If they come to me for help, I will give them all the help I can to reach their goals. But the most important thing is that they work hard and think for themselves.

What is the most important program that you are working on for the women of Bamiyan? Education is the most important program that I am working on now, and will be for some time. Ninety-nine percent of the women in Bamiyan are illiterate, so it is very important to improve the education system here. Years of war have broken the education system.

How does your husband feel about the work that you do? He is supporting me and I think that it is because of his years of support that I now hold a position like this. I thank him for all of his support.

If you were given the opportunity to leave the country, would you go or continue to work for the women of Afghanistan? I will stay here and work for the women of my country as long as I am able to do so. This, I feel, is my duty.

90 ·

Farzana Wahidy, Photojournalist

Suhila Fanoos, Welayet Women's Prison Guard in Central Kabul

فرزانه واحدی

FARZANA WAHIDY,
PHOTOJOURNALIST

"Sometimes the only way to get a true Afghan story is to have an Afghan woman take the photos."

Why is photojournalism important in Afghanistan? Over ninety percent of Afghans are illiterate, so they can't read to get information about their country and the world. I find photojournalism more useful because such a large percentage of my country's population gets their news from looking at photos.

What is the importance of your being a female photojournalist? It is clear that a woman is very open with another woman. To capture a true Afghan story, a story about Afghan women, sometimes the only way to get that story is to have an Afghan woman take the photos.

What does this do for your work, in other words, what would be the difference between your work on a story that involves women and that of an Afghan man? In some cases only women can cover the story like in prisons or hospitals. So if there are no female photojournalists, the story does not get told.

Do people in your life, family and friends, recognize that the job you are doing is an important one? Yes, my father always talks to me about my work; that this is a chance to tell the true story of Afghanistan and that this is a big responsibility and that I should respect it. He tells me that I should do something, not just know about it, but do something about it.

You are a leader in what you are doing, heading down a path few Afghan women have. What do you say to women when they tell you they want to be a photojournalist? When I go to the provinces, some of the women say to me that they would like to be like me; literate, traveling and seeing many places and working. I tell them to study and help their male family members understand how important that is to them.

You could be hurt doing this kind of work, why do you still do it? Some people say to me that if I die doing this work it will be a shame for my family. If I die doing this, it's not a shame for me because I have a big responsibility with this job. If I die doing this work, I will be proud.

The lives of Afghan women are slowly changing. What do you think of the future for Afghan women? I think Afghan women should not be sleeping now. There are reports everywhere that the rights for women are changing, but it is only happening in the big cities. But in the provinces, they are still not aware of the freedoms they have.

What needs to happen to improve this? There need to be more classes for men and for women to teach them the rights of women. We need to change the minds of the men. If this happens, then women's minds will change too.

سهيلا فانوس

SUHILA FANOOS, WELAYET WOMEN'S PRISON GUARD IN CENTRAL KABUL

"I feel deep inside that I am helping these women learn so when they get out they can have a better life."

What do you feel about the "new" Afghanistan that these women will face once they leave your prison? I think that the changes that have taken place over the last few years will help the women of Afghanistan. They will begin to have their own rights. When these women get out of prison, I hope that with my teaching they will be able to find jobs.

How long have you kept the door here at the prison? I have been working at the Welayet prison for eight years.

My primary responsibility is keeping the women prisoners inside. Most of the women are here for three to five years.

Ever had a jailbreak? In my eight years I have never experienced any problems with the prisoners and I am very proud of my job.

The role of women in Afghanistan is changing, how do you see your job playing a part in that? It is a very important job as I also serve as a teacher to the women here. I teach them how to read and write and what is just and wrong. It is a job that holds a great deal of responsibility and I am very proud of it. I feel deep inside that I am helping these women learn so when they get out they can have a better life.

Have you ever been married? I need to be lonely in this job. I am not and probably will never be married while I have this job. It is much easier to do it without a husband. And, I never liked the idea of marriage.

You have seen a lot of women come and go from this prison, what helps them succeed in life once they leave? One thing I always include in my teaching is that they have hope. Hope for something better when they leave this door. I know this works because some women who have left the prison have come back to thank me for what I have done for them.

Lailama Nabizada, Afghan National Army Helicopter Pilot

لیلما نبی زاده

LAILAMA NABIZADA, AFGHAN NATIONAL ARMY HELICOPTER PILOT

"If women were treated the same as men, we might even be better pilots."

How do the men you are flying react when they climb into your helicopter and see that a woman is in the cockpit? I have not gotten many bad reactions. When they see me behind the controls, most of the passengers say encouraging words. They say positive things about me flying and tell me to continue with my job. My sister is also a helicopter pilot and she has even flown President Karzai. He did not say anything to either of us yet though.

Do you think President Karzai does not pay special attention to you and your sister because he accepts you as a pilot like he would any other person? It's good that President Karzai does not give me special treatment because I'm a female pilot, but I think we could use some encouragement.

So maybe there's a lack of encouragement, but what about men making it harder for you than it already is? There used to be bad reactions from men in the past, but now my sister and I don't give them the opportunity. We act very confident and have a courageous air about us so now the bad reactions are much less. We don't give them the time or the opportunity to react badly. If women were treated the same as men, we might even be better pilots.

What are your mother and father like and how did they encourage you? Our father was working for the army before, but now he is retired. Our mother can't read or write, so she encouraged us to do big things with our lives and that we could do whatever we wanted to do.

You are setting a positive example for women in Afghanistan. How do you feel about the future for women in your country? I know that our work is an encouragement to many women and girls, especially when we go to far places. We always tell women that they need to study. This is the most important thing. I think the future for Afghan women is bright. They now know that they need to get an education and they need to better themselves.

Education is an area that needs a great deal of work; what else needs to change for women in Afghanistan? I think that the government needs to encourage the women of this country to work. If they see that women like my sister and I can live a good life by working, it will encourage women to work and better themselves.

How do you feel about the future of Afghan women in the military? There are only a few women who can join the military because most Afghan women are not educated. More women need to go to school and then more women will be able to join the military.

102 ·

Mahmooda Hoseini, Female Mullah

Hamida Jan, Actress / Refugee

Mahgul, Handicraft Worker

Marina Gulbahari, Actress

مارینا کلبهاری

MARINA GULBAHARI, ACTRESS

"I want to keep working on films and one day become a director."

For an Afghan girl to become an actress is a bold move, what made you decide to do it? It was difficult after filming the movie *Osama*. Even after filming for six days I still did not know what the film was about, as I had never acted before. Now, I really like it and am working on more films.

Was your family supportive of your becoming an actress? When I was first approached by the director I was very scared. I asked him what the film was about and he told me it is about women during the Taliban time, my parents agreed that it was okay for me to work on it.

Why did they agree? It was true what the film was showing. That a girl could not study under the Taliban and that for a girl in trouble, her entire family in trouble, she had to pretend that she was a boy so her family could live. When I told this to my family they agreed and now they are happy.

Are you studying now? Now I am going to school and studying. My family did not have the money to pay for the underground girls' schools during the Taliban.

How did you feel when you were playing this role in the movie, as scenes of the film you actually lived through, were you reliving your bad experiences? It is like I started two new lives, first after the Taliban left and then again after I acted in this film. I am happy that I played the role because it showed the realities of Afghan life to people not living in Afghanistan. And it showed how our people suffered.

Afghanistan has gotten better, but there are many things that still need to change. What do you think needs to change the most for women? Lots of things have changed in Afghanistan. Women can go to work; women can take classes. But things still need to change more. For instance, if a woman is asked to act in a movie she only wants to play the role of a mother or a sister. So more things need to change in the film industry in Afghanistan; women need to feel more comfortable and more women need to act.

How have your life and the life of your family changed since being in *Osama*? Before I was in the movie I could not even read and write my name, now I go to school to better myself and my family.

What do you see in your future? I want to continue with my education. I love my English courses, and really want to learn English much better. I want to keep working on films and one day become a director.

"The one thing I need, and all Afghan girls need, is to be more independent."

— Zubaida Akbar, Journalist

Zubaida Akbar, Journalist

Roshan Gul, Beekeeper

HARRISON COUNTY
PUBLIC LIBRARY
105 North Capitol Ave.
Corydon, IN 47112

زبیده اکبر

ZUBAIDA AKBAR, JOURNALIST

**"The one thing I need, and all Afghan girls
need, is to be more independent."**

116 ·

**You are living a very nontraditional life for most Afghan
women. How does your family react to this?** My family is
the only support for me. The reason they help me is that they
are hopeful for change in Afghanistan; they want the role for
women in my country to change. My family wants to be the
first people to start this change.

Have you seen that change taking place? I hope that more
changes will come. There are changes, but there is a need for
so much more to happen.

**As you said there are changes happening, but what still
needs to be done?** The one thing I need, and all Afghan girls
need, is to be more independent. We need the right to make
choices and decisions for ourselves; we should be able to work
for ourselves; we should be able to study for ourselves.

**There are confusing messages out there for Afghan women.
You can see Bollywood posters in many cities that show
Indian women not covering themselves, but women who
walk those streets are told by their husbands and fathers
that they have to cover themselves. Does this confuse
Afghan women?** Any change in Afghanistan cannot be done
quickly. It is not a developed country. We can't make changes
with closed eyes; it is our culture to test everything before
we change. The more freedom we all have over our lives, the
better choices we will make.

What has to be done for the men to make this change? We
need public education that informs people of their freedoms
and their rights; also more trust in one another.

**Do you get frustrated when people from the West tell
Afghan women how to change your society and that it needs
to be done now?** Change is never fast here. When foreigners
first come to Afghanistan they really don't know much about
how things are here. The important thing is to find a starting
point. Everything can't change at once, so it's important to
find the right place to start changing things.

**There will still be problems even as things are getting
better. What do you think those problems will be?** I think
the women are making the problems for themselves. We have
so many opportunities now, but we have to look beyond
ourselves. I am changing, but I am only one woman. It is my
responsibility to help change other women out there, because
if I don't there will only be a small portion of women who
change their ways.

**So, is it part of an Afghan woman's responsibility to help
other Afghan women understand their rights and freedom?**
Of course. If I want to live in this society and have the
freedoms that I deserve, I need to have other people thinking
the same way and willing to fight for me and help me keep my
freedom. If they leave, I have no one to defend me.

روشن گل

ROSHAN GUL, BEEKEEPER

"Now there are a lot of projects to help the women of my country."

This kind of beekeeping is new to Afghanistan and Bamiyan. How did you become involved in this? I am part of a union, men and women, and people came to teach us how to read and write and how to do this job of beekeeping. This is how I learned this job. They gave us the tools to start our own business.

This can be a dangerous line of work, working with bees. Did that concern you? We have a special tool that we were taught to use, a kind of smoke, so they won't sting us. We were taught how to do this properly so we are safe when we take the honey from the bee houses.

Why did you choose to do this job? I needed to find a way to earn money and this was a way to earn money without having to pay a lot to start my business. I hope that I will be able to expand my business in the future. I am still learning, but I think we will get better at this and buy more bees and make more honey.

Who buys your honey? I sell it to local people here in Bamiyan because it is good for many illnesses. Bees are very clean so the honey is very good for stomach problems, for asthma, for women who are pregnant, and for people with kidney stones. We were taught the medicinal uses in our class.

What do you tell other women who tell you they want to be beekeepers? I tell them that this is a good business for them. They can work on their own and help to take care of their family. I encourage them to do this.

What does the future hold for the women of Afghanistan? Everything is getting better since the Taliban has left. That was the important thing to help the future for women, changing the government. Now there are a lot of projects to help the women of my country. This is important because women now can provide for their families and learn new jobs.

What is the one thing that needs to change now for the women of Afghanistan? For us here in Bamiyan, we need more clinics and our school is very far away. This needs to change so our daughters can go to school.

Parwana Ghezel, Ariana Afghan Airlines Flight Attendant

Fareshta Kohistani, United Nations Photographer

ACKNOWLEDGMENTS

Thank you to the brave women in this book who opened their lives and homes for the greater improvement of all Afghan women. To the Akbar family, who has been more than our Afghan family, but the inspiration for this project. To Zubaida and Shaharzad, who worked with us hand-in-hand during this project helping us keep in mind the focus of this book. They joined the project to learn, but they taught more than they realize.

To our families, the Kiviats and the Heidlers, who have endured our absence for long stretches so that *Women of Courage* could be finished. To Lori Hawkins and Eastman Kodak, USA for early and lasting support. To the tireless effort, enthusiasm, and design talent of Matthew McNerney. To George Beylerian for believing in us and the importance of the project, and connecting us with the publisher Gibbs Smith. And lastly to the entire Gibbs Smith team.

Shah Gul, The Beekeeper's (Roshan Gul) Daughter

DISCARD

HARRISON COUNTY PUBLIC LIBRARY

3 MAIN 00105709 C